Jorge *from* A

The Story of Pope Francis for Children

Written by
Marlyn Monge, FSP, and Jaymie Stuart Wolfe

Introduction by
Cardinal Seán Patrick O'Malley, OFM Cap.

Illustrations by
Diana Kizlauskas

Pauline
BOOKS & MEDIA
Boston

Library of Congress Cataloging-in-Publication Data

Monge, Marlyn.
  Jorge from Argentina : the story of Pope Francis for children / written by Marlyn Monge, FSP and Jaymie Stuart Wolfe ; illustrations by Diana Kizlauskas ; introduction by Cardinal Seán Patrick O'Malley.
      pages cm
  ISBN-13: 978-0-8198-4006-6
  ISBN-10: 0-8198-4006-8
  1. Francis, Pope, 1936---Juvenile literature. I. Kizlauskas, Diana, illustrator. II. Title.
  BX1378.7.M66 2013
  282.092--dc23
  [B]
                              2013023103

Introduction by Cardinal Seán Patrick O'Malley, OFM Cap.

Cover design by Mary Joseph Peterson, FSP

Illustrated by Diana Kizlauskas

Written by Marlyn Evangelina Monge, FSP, and Jaymie Stuart Wolfe

Published by Pauline Books & Media, 50 Saint Pauls Avenue, Boston, MA 02130-3491

Printed in the U.S.A.

JFAE VSAUSAPEOILL6-20J13-05586 4006-8

www.pauline.org

Pauline Books & Media is the publishing house of the Daughters of St. Paul, an international congregation of women religious serving the Church with the communications media.

1 2 3 4 5 6 7 8 9   17 16 15 14 13

Contents

Introduction

I'd like to tell you a story about my friend,
Pope Francis. A couple years ago, before he was pope,
I stopped in Argentina on a trip to South America.
Cardinal Jorge Bergoglio invited me to spend some time
with him. We had a wonderful visit with lots of laughs.
I still have great memories of my time with him.
Cardinal Jorge is a good friend—he even gave me a gift!
It was a recording of traditional Argentine music that is
sung at Holy Mass.

Now Pope Francis is a gift for all of us. He loves
Jesus and the Church. He is teaching all of us how to
live out the Gospel in our lives. Pope Francis is simple
and kind, and he *loves* children. So I'd like to invite you
to get to know our Holy Father Francis better.

This book you are about to read is full of interesting stories about Pope Francis's life. You will learn about what happened to him when he was a child and a young adult. You will see how he followed God's plan for him as a Jesuit, a priest, and a bishop. You will get to know Cardinal Jorge from Argentina, and learn how he became our Holy Father.

God always listens to the prayers of children. I hope you will remember to pray for Pope Francis, and ask God to bless him and to help him serve us as pope!

— *Cardinal Seán Patrick O'Malley, OFM Cap.*
Archbishop of Boston

A New Beginning

Mario Bergoglio (bear-GO-lee-o) was a young man. He was standing in a little church dressed in his best clothing. He was waiting for his beautiful bride. Mario thought about all that had happened in the past seven years.

Mario was twenty-four years old when he left northern Italy. He and his parents, Giovanni and Rosa, had sailed to Buenos Aires. They hoped for a better life. Giovanni had been a railroad worker in Italy. It was not easy to earn enough money to support his family there. So they decided to sell their house and join Giovanni's brothers in Argentina.

Argentina is a country in South America where people speak Spanish.

Rosa had sewn their money into the collar of her beautiful fox fur coat. With this money the family would be able to start over in a new land. She wore the coat as they left the ship in spite of the heat. They arrived on a hot, summer morning in January, 1929.

The Bergoglio family was happy to find other Italian immigrants already living in Argentina. Still, they needed to make many changes. At home they spoke Italian. Outside their home, however, they learned to speak in Spanish. There were different customs and traditions, music, and dance. Even the seasons were opposite! Learning so many new things all at once was a challenge. It took patience and a lot of hard work. They were able to do it by God's grace.

As Mario continued to remember, a smile spread over his face. Just a year ago, something happened that changed his life forever. Mario went to Mass at Saint Anthony's church. There he met a lovely young woman, Regina María Sivori. Her family was also from Italy.

Mario and Regina fell in love. Now Mario waited for her at the altar.

Mario's face beamed as he watched Regina walk down the aisle in her beautiful white dress and veil. The happy couple was married in the little church on December 12, 1935. They settled in the Flores neighborhood of Buenos Aires. They lived in a simple house with a lemon tree and a grapefruit tree in the yard. There, they thanked God for the gift of life and the blessing they had found in each other.

Grandma's House

Regina and Mario soon learned that they were going to have a baby. The baby boy was born on December 17, 1936. The proud parents named their son Jorge (HOR-hay) Mario. They often called him by his nickname, Jorgito (hor-HEE-to), or "Little Jorge."

The whole family loved Jorgito. But he was not the youngest Bergoglio for very long. When he was just over a year old, his mother gave birth to another baby boy, Oscar. Jorgito was now a big brother!

"I know that taking care of little ones is a lot of work, Regina," said Jorge's Grandma Rosa. "I'd be

happy to come by in the mornings and take Jorgito
home with me until the afternoon."

Jorgito enjoyed spending time with his grandparents.
Grandma Rosa and Grandpa Giovanni spoke Italian to
each other at home. They also spoke Italian to Jorgito.
So Jorge grew up speaking both Spanish and Italian.

Each day, Grandma Rosa came to pick up Jorge.
All morning Jorge, Grandma Rosa, and Grandpa
Giovanni read and played together. They also ate the

feast Grandma Rosa prepared for lunch every day. Jorgito's grandparents taught him how to pray. They told him stories from the lives of the saints too. Then in the afternoon, he returned home.

On the outside, Jorge's house was nothing special. It was just a small place with two fruit trees. But inside, the love and faith of the growing Bergoglio family made it a wonderful place to be a child.

Happy Days

Jorge soon started school at *Colegio Misericordia* (Mercy School) in his neighborhood. There he was taught by sisters who belonged to the Daughters of Our Lady of Mercy.

Jorge enjoyed collecting stamps. He also had fun playing with Oscar and the other children at school. And Jorge had lots of energy! Sister Dolores, one of his teachers, laughed when she saw him "study" math. Bouncing and laughing, Jorgito jumped up and down the stairs as he recited his multiplication tables aloud.

Jump, "Two times two is four!" Jump, "Two times three is six!" Jump, "Two times four is eight!" Jorge did this over and over again, smiling and laughing the whole time. He never grew tired of jumping!

When Jorgito was old enough, Sister Dolores helped to prepare him for first Holy Communion. Jorge, Oscar, and the other children learned about Mass together. Sister Dolores taught them that when the priest said the words of consecration, God changed the bread and wine into the real Body and Blood of Jesus. They also learned the Ten Commandments and many other things that would help them choose between right and wrong.

"Children, the best thing you can do is to pray," said Sister Dolores. "Pray to God when you have decisions to make. And don't forget to ask Mother Mary to help you always stay close to her Son."

Jorge was so excited he could hardly wait. He prayed every day that God would open his heart to receive Jesus. He loved the Blessed Mother and prayed a Hail Mary often asking her to help him be a good boy.

Before he knew it, the day Jorge had eagerly awaited arrived. Jorgito knelt at the altar rail next to his brother Oscar. The priest approached and held the consecrated

Host up and said, "The Body of Christ." Jorge responded quickly and solemnly, "Amen," and opened his mouth. He couldn't stop smiling. He had received Jesus, and his heart jumped just as his feet did when he bounced on the stairs.

Helping Hands

Like most boys in Argentina, Jorge was a soccer fan. But he liked playing basketball with his father and friends even more. He also played card games with his parents. On Saturday afternoons, Jorge listened to opera on the radio with his mother and brothers. Jorge didn't have a lot of time to play, however. There was always studying or homework to do for school, or help needed around the house.

As Jorge grew, so did his family. At twelve years old, he was the oldest of five children. But after the birth of the youngest Bergoglio child, Jorge's mother became paralyzed from the waist down. She was no longer able

to keep up with household tasks by herself. "Boys," said Mr. Bergoglio, "we all need to do more to help your mother. Jorge, you are the oldest. It is important that you set a good example."

So during the day, Mrs. Bergoglio did as much as she could to prepare the family's dinner. She cleaned and cut vegetables and meat. She also got together everything needed for cooking. When Jorge and his two brothers came home from school, she was waiting for them in the kitchen. The boys followed their mother's instructions, and finished making dinner together.

Because he was the oldest, Jorge did most of the cooking on the stove. He really enjoyed it! They all hoped that their mother would be well again. Still, this daily time together in the kitchen was full of joy. It also gave Jorge and his brothers the chance to learn how to cook for themselves.

Going to Work

In time, Mrs. Bergoglio's health did improve. When Jorge was thirteen, Mr. Bergoglio felt that his oldest son no longer needed to help at home.

"Jorge, now that you are old enough, I think it is time for you to get a part-time job. You can learn a lot from trying to balance school and work," said his dad. The family didn't need the money Jorge would be able to earn. Still, Mr. Bergoglio wanted to teach his son the value and dignity of work. "I may be able to get you a job at the sock factory. But you won't be keeping the accounts like I do."

Jorge's days were full. In the morning he worked from 7:00 a.m. until 1:00 p.m. Then after eating lunch he went to school until 8:00 p.m. If he finished his homework, Jorge met his friends for some fun. Though it was a challenge, Jorge was learning that it was possible to balance all the important things in his life.

During his first two years at the sock factory, Jorge worked cleaning the floors and the equipment. The third year, his boss gave him some administrative work to do.

Since he was studying chemistry at school, however, Jorge left his job at the factory and began to work at a laboratory. It was good have a job that allowed him to put his studies into practice.

One day his boss at the lab noticed how quickly he finished his work. "Jorge," she asked, "did you really do *all* of the chemical tests?"

"No, not all," Jorge sheepishly replied. "But I don't really know why I should analyze this sample when the result will be like all the ones I did earlier today."

His boss stopped him and said, "Jorge, all work is worth trying your best. Take pride in each thing you do, even when it seems small."

After she spoke to him, Jorge did a complete test of every sample. Work not only put a little money in his pocket, it also made him feel good about what he was doing.

As he closed the door of the laboratory Jorge saw some friends. Waving, he went off to spend some time with them before going to school.

An Unexpected Discovery

Wow! It looks like it's going to be a great day! thought seventeen-year-old Jorge as he left his house. The sun was shining and there was a nice warm breeze. It was September 21, the Day of the Student, and there was no school. Jorge planned to spend the holiday with his friends. They would have lots of fun—having a picnic, playing a bit of soccer, and perhaps even going dancing later! Jorge really liked to dance the *milonga* with some of the girls he knew. *Yes! It is definitely going to be an awesome day!*

On his way to the train station, Jorge decided it would be a good idea to stop at St. Joseph church in his neighborhood to pray. He often liked to begin his day quietly with the Lord. And today he had plenty of time before meeting his friends.

Sunshine came in through the beautiful stained glass windows. It made colorful patterns of light on the floor. Jorge noticed a priest seated in the church, a priest he had never met before. After he said a little prayer thanking God for the day ahead, Jorge and the priest began to talk. Father Duarte spoke about God and about life. As they continued to talk, Jorge was moved by the priest's words and decided to ask for the sacrament of Reconciliation.

After his confession Jorge spent a bit more time in prayer. He had started to sense a growing excitement within himself. Jorge felt as if God was giving him a great gift and that filled him with joy and deep peace. *I want to . . . no . . . I MUST become a priest.* He had never thought about it before, but now Jorge felt strongly that God was calling him to help people in their relationship with God, just as Father Duarte had done for him.

Jorge left the church. But instead of meeting his friends at the train station Jorge returned home to reflect on what he had discovered—his life's vocation!

An Important Choice

Jorge prayed and waited. He wanted to be sure that God really was calling him to become a priest. In the meantime, Jorge finished high school and continued working at the laboratory.

In time, Jorge became more certain about his vocation. He spoke first with his father. "I want to be a priest. It's a call my heart has been waiting for. I didn't even realize it, Papa," he explained. Mr. Bergoglio was pleased. He asked Jorge only if he was sure of his choice.

Although faith was important to Jorge's mother, she was not happy to hear of her son's plans. "I can't see you entering the seminary now, Jorge. I think you should wait. This decision has come too fast." For several years, Mrs. Bergoglio struggled to accept her oldest son's choice.

Grandma Rosa approached Jorge's news differently. "If God is calling you, then go. But remember that if you change your mind, the doors of your home will always be open. No one will think that you failed." Jorge was relieved and felt free to do what God was asking of him.

When he was nineteen, Jorge decided to enter the seminary of his archdiocese. There he would begin the studies and prayer that would lead him to priesthood.

Three years later, however, Jorge became very ill. He was admitted to the hospital with a high fever and difficulty breathing. One of his lungs was severely infected and a large part of it had to be removed.

Jorge's worried mother stayed with him at the hospital for long hours. Sister Dolores, the teacher who had prepared Jorge for his first Holy Communion, also

came. Many family members and friends told him that
the pain and sickness would soon be over. But Sister
Dolores said something very different. "You are
following Christ and sharing the pain he felt on the
cross." These words gave Jorge courage and strength.

Next Steps

After he was well again, Jorge made another choice. He decided to go to a different seminary. Jorge joined the Jesuits (JEH-zoo-its). Jesuits are members of the religious order called the Society of Jesus. Saint Ignatius of Loyola and his friends began the Society of Jesus in 1534.

Jorge liked the Jesuits. He was impressed by their commitment to the Church and their mission work. He was also drawn to the idea of being like a soldier for Christ. The Jesuits are very educated men who work in many different fields. Some are even scientists, doctors, professors, or lawyers!

"Becoming a Jesuit priest will take a long time, Jorge," the novice master said. "My job is to help you learn how to live as a Jesuit. It will be nearly ten years before you are finished. "

"Then we should start right away, Father," Jorge replied. Jorge looked forward to the journey. He was sure that he was following God's plan for his life. He was also happy to be able to study and pray more.

Jorge learned about the Jesuit way of life. He took his first religious vows in 1960. He was twenty-four years old. As a follower of Saint Ignatius, he promised to live in community, serve the Church, and reach out to the world. And, as all Jesuits do, Jorge promised not to seek positions of power or authority.

Several years would pass before Jorge could be ordained a priest. It would be even longer before he could make his final vows as a Jesuit. During this time of preparation, Jorge finished his studies and taught classes. Most of all Jorge deepened his friendship with Jesus through prayer and the spiritual exercises of Saint Ignatius.

A Priest Forever

Jorge was almost thirty-three years old. After many years of study, the day of Jorge's ordination was quickly approaching. He would soon be a priest! Jorge knew that he needed to find quiet and peace. So much was happening. He slipped into the Jesuit chapel to pray. There he sat thinking about his life. Jorge wrote in his journal the things that God was helping him to believe and accept.

I believe that throughout my life God has always loved me and, in particular, on that spring day in September God invited me through Father Duarte to follow him as a priest. . . . I believe others are good, and I should love them without fear. . . .

I believe in Mary, my mother, who will never leave me alone.... Jorge wrote and wrote.

When he finished, Jorge had written down thirteen things he believed. He signed his name at the bottom, folded the paper, and put it in his prayer book. It would remind him of how God was calling him to live.

Jorge was ordained a few days later at Mass on December 13, 1969. Archbishop Ramón José Castellano laid his hands on Jorge's head. *"You are a priest forever..."* The words echoed in Jorge's heart. *Thank you, Jesus! Mary, my mother, please pray for me. Help me to be a faithful priest who will love all the people God sends,* Jorge prayed. After receiving the sacrament of Holy Orders, Jorge stood tall. His face showed how very happy he was. He was now Father Jorge Bergoglio, a priest, forever.

Not long afterward he was made novice master. His task was to help young men discover if God was calling them to be Jesuits. On April 22, 1973, Father Jorge made his own final profession as a Jesuit. He vowed to live a poor, obedient, and chaste life—and to completely obey the pope in matters of mission.

After his final vows Father Jorge was very busy. In addition to being novice master, he had many other responsibilities. He taught classes and helped organize school events. He even cooked for the students on the weekends. When possible, Father Jorge made time to visit the sisters who had taught him as a child. Sister Dolores was excited to hear about all that he was doing. Once she said to another sister, "Wait and we'll see. Father Jorge will become someone very important one day."

Troubles and Terror

A few months later, Father Jorge was asked to lead all the Jesuits of Argentina. He served as the provincial superior from 1973 until 1979. These were very difficult times in Argentina.

Cruel leaders took control of the government. Ordinary people suffered terrible crimes. Anyone who did not support them was at risk. Artists and writers, priests and nuns, students and journalists who worked with the poor were kidnapped and tortured. Many were killed, and everyone was afraid.

During the years of Argentina's "Dirty War," Father Jorge had difficult decisions to make. *Do I openly*

oppose them, Lord? Or should I do what I can to help in secret?
His prayers were filled with questions.

Father Jorge worked quietly against the violence.
He hid many people from harm, and helped others to
escape. He even gave his own identity papers to a
man who looked like him so that the man could leave
Argentina!

Then two Jesuit priests were suspected of working
against the government. Father Jorge tried to change

their assignments in order to protect them. It did not work. Father Orlando and Father Franz were arrested and tortured.

While the two priests were in prison, Father Jorge had another idea. He called a priest who knew one of the government leaders. "Can I take your place to celebrate Mass for the general in charge?" Father Jorge asked. *If I go myself,* he thought, *I can ask the general to let the Jesuits go. Perhaps he would release them.* The other priest agreed. Finally, good news came. The two priests were found wandering the countryside alive.

In 1980 his time as superior ended. Two years later, the terror of the war came to a close. Father Jorge was glad that the worst was over. He felt more than ready for the new challenges—and joys—ahead.

An Airport Meeting

In May of 1992 Father Jorge received a telephone call. It was from the pope's representative in Argentina.

"Father Jorge, I'd like to meet with you to talk about a few things," the archbishop said.

"Certainly," Father Jorge replied. It was not unusual for the archbishop to ask Father Jorge's opinion.

"The problem is that I am only going to be in Cordoba for a few hours," Archbishop Ubaldo added. "Can you meet me at the airport while I wait for my next flight?"

Father Jorge was happy to help. The two men met at the gate. While the archbishop waited for his plane, they talked about what was happening in the Church and in Argentina. They even spoke about which priests might someday be a good choice to serve the people as a bishop.

Before long, the attendant announced that it was time for all passengers to board the plane. Archbishop Ubaldo picked up his small bag in one hand and held his boarding pass in the other. Just before they said goodbye, he turned to Father Jorge and said, "Oh, there is one more thing I need to tell you. Pope John Paul has decided which priests will be Argentina's new bishops."

"I'm sure that whoever the Holy Father has chosen will be good and wise shepherds for God's people," said Father Jorge confidently.

"I agree," the archbishop replied. "The Pope has chosen someone for Buenos Aires who is simple, very humble, loves the people—and is quite wise, too."

"Someone like that is just who we need. May I ask who he is?"

Archbishop Ubaldo looked at Father Jorge and smiled. "You," he answered. "The public announcement will be made by the end of the month. Your ordination will be after that."

With a pat of his hand on Father Jorge's shoulder the archbishop turned and boarded the plane. Father Jorge was shocked! It was the last thing he expected to hear.

Father Jorge knew in his heart that he had never sought or wanted to be bishop. But he took his vow of obedience to the pope very seriously. He would serve as Pope John Paul II asked. In his heart he quickly prayed, *"O Mother of God, help me to do your Son's will."*

Father Jorge became Bishop Jorge, an assistant bishop of Buenos Aires, on June 27, 1992.

One with the People

Bishop Jorge wanted to remain an assistant bishop. But when the Archbishop of Buenos Aires died, Pope John Paul II had a different idea.

On February 28, 1998, the Holy Father made Bishop Jorge the Archbishop of Buenos Aires. Three years later he became a cardinal. Cardinals are advisors to the pope.

As the leader of more than two million Catholics, Cardinal Archbishop Jorge was very busy. His calendar was filled with countless meetings, talks, retreats, and much more. Still, each year he made time for something special. On the anniversary of his first Holy Communion, Cardinal Jorge returned to his childhood neighborhood church. There he celebrated Mass where he had first received Jesus.

Although archbishops are very important, Cardinal Jorge didn't want to be treated differently. "I know the Archbishop of Buenos Aires usually lives in a fancy house," Cardinal Jorge said to his staff. "But I want to stay close to the people and live the way they do. All I need is a bed, a desk, and a bookcase," he added. "And I won't need anyone to drive me around. I can take the train or bus."

Deep inside Jorge was still a simple priest. He was an ordinary Jesuit who lived his vows every day. The people of Buenos Aires were happy to know that Cardinal Jorge cared about them. He was their shepherd. He made time to talk with them while he rode the bus or train. He would even accept a sip of *mate*, a hot drink popular in Argentina. People share *mate* with each other, and drink it through a straw from the same gourd.

Remaining close to the people he served, Cardinal Jorge led by example. He cared for the needs of those who were poor or forgotten. The way he lived encouraged others to do the same.

Sadness, and a New Shepherd

Everyone knew that Pope John Paul II had been suffering for a very long time. The Holy Father could no longer walk. His hands shook. His face looked worn. By the time Easter came in 2005, he couldn't even speak.

Cardinal Jorge was sad to see the Holy Father struggle. He knew that soon he would have to travel to Rome. There, he would join the other cardinals to elect a new Holy Father. But for now, he just prayed. *Lord, give your peace to Pope John Paul II, watch over your Church, the people of Buenos Aires, and the whole world.*

On April 2, Pope John Paul II lay dying. People could see the lights of the pope's apartment through the curtains from Saint Peter's Square. Crowds from around the world gathered below his window to pray for him. In the twenty-six years he had been pope, John Paul II had given so much of himself. Now that his time on earth was almost done, thousands and thousands of people wanted to express their gratitude. They wanted to show him how much they loved him one last time. Even larger crowds came to Rome for his funeral.

The cardinals met in Rome to begin the conclave (CON-clayv), the process of electing a new pope. Before they entered the Sistine (sis-TEEN) Chapel, they asked the Holy Spirit for wisdom and guidance. There were many men who would make a good shepherd for the Church. Some even thought Cardinal Jorge might be chosen!

Once again people came to Saint Peter's Square. They waited for white smoke to appear. That is the signal that a new pope had been elected. After the first few votes, the small chimney puffed only black smoke. But then, the white smoke came! People rushed to the square to see who the new pope was.

The cardinals, of course, already knew. They had elected Cardinal Joseph Ratzinger from Germany. Now he would be known as Pope Benedict XVI. Cardinal Jorge couldn't have been happier. He had known Pope Benedict XVI for many years. He trusted that God had given the Church a shepherd who would guard Christ's sheep, and spread his love to everyone. "I pledge to you, Holy Father, my obedience and loyalty," Cardinal Jorge said. He bowed to kiss the new pope's ring. Outside the crowds were cheering in anticipation.

Miracles with Jesus

Back in Argentina Cardinal Jorge continued to serve his people. Every year, Cardinal Jorge worked with parents, deacons, and priests to make the Day of the Child special.

On October 21, 2011, thousands of children gathered. The weather was perfect—not too hot and not too cold. Balloons and games filled the *Parque Roca,* and people dressed as giant marionettes to tell the story of Pinocchio. The children watched with wide eyes as the huge wooden puppet with a wooden heart did a lot of nasty things. Some magicians tried to change Pinocchio's heart into a human heart that was able to

know right from wrong. But though they tried and tried, the magicians couldn't change Pinocchio's wooden heart into a real one. At that point in the story the puppets stopped, and Cardinal Jorge continued the story.

"Magic can't change anyone's heart," Cardinal Jorge explained. Then looking at the crowd of children with love he said, "But if magicians can't change a person's heart, who is the only one who can?"

The children all shouted back, "Jesus can!"

"Today we come to ask Jesus to change our hearts so that we can do good," Cardinal Jorge continued. "When we do good, miracles can happen. Boys and girls, did you know that with Jesus you and I can also do miracles? Making a sad person smile is a miracle. Being with a grandparent who is feeling lonely or giving some food to someone who is hungry is also a miracle."

Everyone in the stadium smiled and clapped. Cardinal Jorge loved seeing how happy the children were. As children were leaving with their parents at the end of a fun-filled day, Cardinal Jorge could hear a little brother and sister ask their mom, "Mama, do you think we can do what Cardinal Jorge said and help others? Can Jesus help us to do miracles?" The mother's answer was drowned out by all the noise but Cardinal Jorge could see her smile and nod. *Thank you, Jesus,* he prayed. *Thank you for helping me tell people about how you work in our lives. May these children grow to know you better day by day.*

Surprising News

"Did you hear?" "Is it true?" Everyone wanted to know. After eight years as pope, Benedict XVI had unexpectedly announced his decision to resign. In just a few weeks, on February 28, 2013, Pope Benedict would leave Vatican City and no longer serve as the leader of the Church.

Hardly anyone could believe the news. While he was not the first pope to leave office this way, it hadn't happened for six hundred years. No one was sure how things would take place, where Pope Benedict would live, what we would call him—or when a new pope would be chosen.

"*Buenos días*," Cardinal Jorge said as his younger sister answered the telephone.

"Jorge!" said Maria Elena, with both excitement and concern in her voice. "Are you getting ready to leave for Rome again?"

"*Sí*," he said as he packed his scarlet red cassock into a suitcase. Even though he had been a cardinal for twelve years, Cardinal Jorge hardly ever wore it. He always preferred clothes that were less fancy and formal. "Don't worry; I'll be back in a few weeks. Hopefully the conclave won't take very long." He hung up the phone and then changed into the new shoes a few friends had bought him for the trip. He had worn his old pair for quite some time and now they were pretty shabby.

Before he left, Cardinal Jorge stopped by the newsstand to let the newspaper man know that he would be gone for a while and wouldn't be picking up the paper every day as he usually did. Then Cardinal Jorge took a bus to the airport and boarded a plane for Rome.

Bowing and Blessing

One-hundred-fifteen cardinals came from all over the world. They were not in any rush to begin the conclave. Instead, they met for several days. This gave them a chance to thank Pope Emeritus (eh-MARE-i-tus) Benedict XVI for all he had done. On March 12, 2013, they were ready to choose a new pope.

The Cardinals walked into the Sistine Chapel, just as they had eight years before. Voting would be held four times a day until a new pope was chosen. As each cardinal cast his vote, he prayed that the Holy Spirit would guide him. The ballots would be counted aloud.

On the second day of the conclave, Cardinal Jorge began to realize that more than a few cardinals had voted for him. After all the ballots had been counted, there were enough votes to make him the new pope.

"Do you accept election?" the cardinal in charge asked him.

"Yes," he answered quietly, shocked at what had just happened.

"What name will we call you?"

"Francis," responded Cardinal Jorge, "in honor of Saint Francis of Assisi. Saint Francis loved the poor and rebuilt the Church." None of the 265 popes before him had ever chosen that name.

No one expected the conclave to end so soon. Everyone was surprised when white smoke streamed from the small chimney that evening. The bells of all the churches in Rome began to ring. Thousands of people rushed to Saint Peter's Square to see the new pope. Millions watched on television or the Internet. Everyone was surprised when they found out who had been chosen: Cardinal Jorge Mario Bergoglio, from Argentina —Pope Francis.

He stepped out onto the balcony in the white cassock only popes wear. The people cheered loudly.

Pope Francis paused to take it all in. Then he surprised everyone again. The Holy Father led everyone around the world in praying a Hail Mary, an Our Father, and a Glory be. Then, before he blessed the people, the new Holy Father asked them to give him their blessing. Pope Francis bowed humbly on the balcony. The crowd fell silent as they asked God to bless him. "Good evening!" he said rising. "I will see you tomorrow. Have a good rest!"

Much to his surprise, Cardinal Jorge was now Pope Francis. The first pope from the Americas would not be going home to Argentina any time soon.

Go and Make Disciples

Flags from every nation waved in the Brazilian sky. Three million young people had come from all over the world to Rio di Janeiro (REE-oh day-juh-NER-oh) to participate in World Youth Day 2013. They came to pray, to learn, and to serve. They came to celebrate their faith together, and to experience Jesus and his Church. The excitement was everywhere!

Pope Francis was excited too. It was his very first trip to another country since he became pope. It was also a chance to return to South America. On July 25, he stood before the eager crowd. "I am happy to be here to welcome you!" beamed Pope Francis. "I don't have gold or silver," he continued, "but I bring you the most precious thing I have: Jesus Christ."

While he was in Brazil, Pope Francis did many things to show people how much God loves them. He met with prisoners and visited a neighborhood where many poor people live. And, of course, he spent time with all the young people. *This is why I wanted to be a priest, Jesus*, Pope Francis prayed. *I love to serve your people.*

As he made his way around the city, a nine year old boy managed to get close to Pope Francis's white popemobile. The boy told the Holy Father that he wanted to become a priest. "Today your dream begins to become real," Pope Francis said to him. "I will pray for you, but you must also pray for me."

After several days of celebrating their faith, it was almost time for all the young people and the pope to go home. The highpoint of the week came with a Saturday night prayer vigil and Mass on Sunday morning. There were so many people that the crowd filled the beach for four miles.

During the Mass the Holy Father spoke about following Christ without fear. "Jesus did not say 'if you feel like it' or 'if you have time,'" Pope Francis exclaimed with joy. "Jesus said 'Go and make disciples.'" As the crowd cheered, Pope Francis smiled and prayed in his heart that all the young people around the world would not be afraid to tell others about God. "My dear young people," he continued, "Christ is counting on you! The Church is counting on you! The Pope, too, is counting on you!"